PROVOCATIONS

Recent Books by Ray DiPalma

The Jukebox of Memnon
Potes & Poets Press, 1988

Raik
Roof Books, 1989

Night Copy
Stele, 1990

5 Ink Drawings & 5 Poems
[with Elizabeth DiPalma]
Stele, 1990

Mock Fandango
Sun & Moon Press, 1991

Metropolitan Corridor
Zasterle Press, 1992

Numbers and Tempers
Sun & Moon Press, 1993

27 Octobre 29 Octobre
Format américain, 1993

Hôtel des Ruines
[with lithographs by Alexandre Delay]
La Collection Porterie/Éditions Royaumont, 1993

Symptoms of the Absolute
Privately printed, 1993

Platinum Replica
[with drawings by Elizabeth DiPalma]
Stele, 1994

PROVOCATIONS

Ray DiPalma

Potes & Poets Press
Elmwood, CT
1994

Copyright © 1994 by Ray DiPalma

Grateful acknowledgement is made
to the editors of the following magazines
where versions of some of these poems originally appeared:
*American Letters & Commentary, Exqusite Corpse, Hole,
O.ARS, Salt Lick, 6ix* and *Stele.*

Thanks to the New York Foundation for the Arts
for a grant that was of help in writing these poems.

Cover Design: Elizabeth DiPalma

ISBN 0-937013-55-2

PROVOCATIONS

Then the language doesn't get used up

A bent crowd

Inside language

Nor is it bluer or hybrid

Wrapped in time-honored bars of light

The work of a mason and a nomad

THE ONUS IN NOUNS

What happens within the progress of thought when words
Are applied
What happens against the progress of thought when words
Are applied

Tilth thorn and thistle
The sky in the pond

Curious expression: dead for a while
Which way does it face
What does it *expect*

Hearing what was said in the moment of memory
What was said did not originate with the sayer
Made the memory made out of words

Hearing what the memory made
Saying what the hearing that the memory made

The sky is never invisible whatever is held or planned against it. With its contact the sky is always a place to start. While waiting and so acknowledged waiting ideas eventually come, almost erasing the flawed initiative of the past and deepening the crease between the eyes and just above the bridge of the nose.

Ja, Oui Da, Yes, Si . . . the soil is pause from place to soil: *to place from place* and *place to place.* Flat stones at the entrance of the tunnel. Separation in the ink.

Time's hours spread to appear a projection . . . a protection. Spread into, spread among, spread out, spread along: these could also be called administrative difficulties if one is to believe in tangents of discourse as might be undertaken here and now at this moment of horizon.

On this very night

On this same stretch of road

In the same dense fog

Consequent transparency
Who after whom is who
After *all* or a part of same

As one and one: two ... three
Vagrant shadows
The time spent making decisions like walking under water

That impatient clarity that reveals nothing
[That] framing [that] is balance
And a reasonable notion of falseness ... to discern shape

Lessons of three by two
Will you participate
For three by three: suspicion forestalled

The plod of intentionality every pause
An answer given [ ] 10 syllables before
The question is formed

An ineluctable progression plucked from the strange

A nuance met

Darkness and disguised vibrations arranged this way

Music

Emphasis on this spite to qualify solution

Mass is equation

Initiatives

But to have:

But somehow:

But long enough:

But already:

But the idea:

Uninitiated

Was it a failed arabesque before you were caught in the sunlit trap

Who wants to know

Was it architecture

No it was carpentry but who wants to know

Was it a fragment

It was enough

Who wants to know

Future predicates

Fugitive predicates

The unavoidable secret

Blankness

The shadow of the pilgrim's foot

Where white cancels red or black

Smoke

As well as many ups and downs and alongs

Varnish

The next word not the last not foreshadowed

The breakfast fortune cookie:

"You may attend a party where strange customs prevail."

This is not a double dream but an absorbing if somewhat as yet shapeless complement of earnest moments of addition. There never was intended a point B to follow a point A or a point X to mark the spot or a point C to flow smoothly from point A's bearing on point B's natural inclination to devolve upon what point C might anticipate in the way of points D through Z.

The discipline of patterns and patter need not be either conclusive, inclusive, or, simpatico. In character, out of character (well, maybe, that would be all right), with character, by means of a character, a mask assumed, a voice adopted, a little hitch put into the stride, some shading here or there, chiaroscuro, crayon and silverpoint, oil stick, pastel, pencil, pen and ink—or light.

Will others find some suspended inflection in which certain syllables might be supplanted by certain other syllables with vowels replacing consonants at particular and very specific intervals in order that a code might be created, a gloss might be perpetrated, or cryptic isolated points articulated by means of a series of new alphabets based on mirror writing and Cyrillic letter shapes, traditional marks of punctuation placed in the middle of words to confound and amuse, and what might be considered traditional aims shedding their substantive intent by default when certain "docks of grace" are attained?

Idleness and rage

Literary words

A disputatious side emerges

The sky is reflected off the water not on the water

Enough said

Turning aside to accommodate a desired stillness

Once the center is found how flex a radius

About now another anomaly

Swallows the road

I don't understand what you want to know

THE KEEN OX, *OR*
THE ART OF THE ENGINEER

Calculated evolved an excursion in manner
The apostrophic substance arrived at algebraically
Not allegory rather dehiscence

Paradox laid over hypocrisy
Waiting then for the light to shine
And renew the burden

Vit, cheri, vit, cheri, vit, Vit, VIT
Push and pull until it sounds like victory
Vit, cheri, VIT, Vit, vit

The paper dyed black
The burden of configuration
Tapped out of the light

Instinctive intervals
(The reduction of a head in movement
To bare lines) put to use in memory's query

On the screen one square hole 4" x 4" containing
Words from ¼" to 3" in length

The box on the screen beneath the 4" limit begins to resemble a notch

No words allowed

Just the words

In small caps

NO WORDS ALLOWED

Measurements accurate to ¹⁄₁₆"

It makes its turns not on a hunch but where the telling stretches the shine. Gray visitor, are you shining me on? There are tidings and small shadows on the far wall of the cave but on the wrong side of the fire so the light must be coming from somewhere else. Who are you and where are you standing with that lantern, torch, or burning log? Is your hair on fire? Not such a good symbol. Everything's in profile due to absent-mindedness. There is a wrinkle of permanent resignation in your voice if not on your tongue when I hear you say "What next?" Almost a flattened numbness... almost.

CARTE DE VISITE

That creature's not been transformed but, rather, spiked on a tattered falsetto. Mirrored light reaches into the shadows. No further than that. He, she, it, they all sleep in that brown darkness wishing it were blue. Vagueness accrues as well as civility. Every artifice had a case. Slogans on behalf of the shrouded dragon. Another use for uncertainty. Some luster and chill in the tropic of glint. But one name keeps cropping up. I was once asked if we were on good terms. Though we spoke on the phone, the inquisitor was seeking more than information. She had a fear to celebrate. And stopped singing.

No it couldn't have been something I did
So then it must have been something I said
Then it must have been something I did

Take two
Since it must have been something I said that
Made it something I did no distinctions now
Something I said and did who else to blame

Take three
But it couldn't have been something that I
So it must have been something that you
No more none not any of this you or I or we

THE SPEE IN SPEECH

Number
is the escape from length
to the attribution of pace
and lure
piling out

Not attributes
or attributions
but *to the attribution*
from that de-
cision counted *from*

Like the voice
the river
is effort

"AND WHERE DID PLORNISH LIVE"

In 1972 Asa spoke to me about
A paper merchant in Bleeding Heart Yard
Who sold his stock by the sheet by the quire by the ream
Handling each sheet with utmost care as he presented it
To any prospective customer folios handmade watermarked
Foolscap by the pound
For *Time Being* we used end lots of what was around Trigram
Then situated in Southwark near The George
Ticketboard used for endpapers elsewhere did for our cover
'He lived at the last house in Bleeding Heart Yard,
And his name was over a little gateway.'

Thin-out, cancel, and comfort

An apotheosis that is perennial
Where 'where' is when
And 'when' is

Inside the glory of all directions at once

How else describe a light so intense

Without making clear

Of necessity what might change around

The ravels of melancholy

That brought us finger in hand to this point in time

I thank you for everything

Better gracious than grateful

Ambition can rarely accommodate laughter unless
It be the nervous variety
Clotted behind the tongue

Eyes averted

Like yesterday and tomorrow what are these now

Anything else

The responsibility that bears isolation

The answer that asks

Who wants to know

Like is not like

The diffidence in foreboding

That is something that is reached

Distinct from being arrived at

Turning out from the propagating hollow

Idealized in the reappraisal of such gesture

When who asks who wants to know

Nondescript intimate and phantom

Birds at their stations

The view is admirable

What sort of birds do you keep, admiral?

There seems to be that much more distance in the weather these days. Must be the music I've been playing . . . at least in part. Won't see a bird for days then suddenly the woods behind the barn are full of cardinals, starlings, blue jays, house finches, nuthatches, crows, titmice, blackbirds, goldfinches, red-tail hawks, Canada geese, blue heron and gray . . . then the saw-toothed options of memory and the recondite comforts of incunabula, elephant folio and sweet caporal. Ready wraiths and ancient stuff at the shoulder and under the nose . . . smooth thumb tucked under the huge page's corner anticipatory to guiding the entire hand along the sheet's fore-edge. The weight of the page midway up brings me to my feet to fold it over and discover what might next be there.

A NAIL THROUGH A BISCUIT

Where the page began
With a name that hadn't
Been heard for quite some time

There was an ochre halo behind
A careful series of color bands
Reds blues greens yellows

Out of gradation but arranged and
Separated by a series of thin blue-black lines
Numbered and alternating right and left

In an ancient Arabic script
A small spur shot from thick to thin
From the top of the one giving it

The look of an inverted V
The two flared back from left to right
From beneath the curve of its upper segment

The two arcs of the three were nearly
Of exact size and opened only slightly
Barely touching and angled downward where they met the line

The four was tapered sharply and extended from a bold
Central line suggesting a tree or rather a sacrificial knife
The angled bowl of the five seemed to hang from a broken dart

Betrayed opened-up

Betrayed closed-off

Distance ... the distances coincident with illusion

Young clouds unconfused

And am and these are—the fold

Be-*tres*-ed—exemplum [1][2][3]—taken through

Allegorical scruple

Be-*tres*-ed—exemplum [1][2][3]—taken through—kept the same

Parallel thoughts but isolated as such with the *along* of taken through

What the stress of [2] holds back in its angle—as though about to strike

None of this must go into a letter.

That is where records are falsified or intentionally misinterpreted.

Which line of works suits your fancy?

Who wants to know?

[Space] [Dot Dot Dot] [Space]

Who's asking 'Who wants to know'?

Could some of this find its way into a letter?

The is in missive and the I've.

Just points, then, in time. Is, I am, I've.

Who wants to know?

The old pause
to wipe the crumbs
from the brain
or to bake a new loaf

Fraught with
macro and micro
made desolate by
the stillness in both

[What you see is
what you are [to get]
Til's last name was
Eulenspiegel—Owlglass]

I've strayed for notes
confusing the forgotten
with necessity and polarizing
them both with pause

You stoke your furnace
bank the fires in your oven
noncommittal as bees in winter
gnawing on the hive

Squaring the circle
with the spider's vertical drop
a favorite wall
and the corner of this page

Notchbook not notebook
hornbook and matchbook
bankbook cookbook and
logbook sketchbook and

The resolution of resolves
what has been put here
put forth . . . brought forth
to be put forth

Who wants to know
remoteness is anything
imaginable known from
assailable or for and

As well as might be
and as well as not

He saw no one coming so he went himself.

Asked for a conclusion, he paused long enough to be heard.

He saw no one coming so he went himself.

A+B = C

A [<] [>] B = C

From here to [t]here = C

I hear someone coming.

Could you make something for me?

Version #3

Between medium and large

Who decided it was a more dramatic shift between black and white?

It's just gray.

$35.00 per piece per color

Could you decide in the time allotted?

Could you decide out of what it should be made?

Including the brass tacks?

Inclusive of same

Hanging punctuation

πr^2 is available

And this shoebox full of other stuff I've got on hand

Extra for deluxe and any damages

When we rest we lie horizontally; naturally the feeling of rest comes to us when we see a quiet, well-composed landscape portrayed in a horizontal shape. It should appeal to the observer in such a way as to cause him or her to say, "Hell, I wish I were at that spot," because the spot looks restful to him or her and he or she pictures him or herself away from his or her cares, taking it easy under the trees. I say to hell with both or either. Just make sure you use a filter to catch whatever clouds there may be in the scene.

1
Me about
On luster
Until
The wedding

2
The song
Hasn't arrived
But that's
This road

3
Who owns
The night
We own
The night

4
I could make
A list
That's how
It all began

5
The transient dwarf
Is speaking his
Interludes . . . they
Need no secrets

A painted wall
two painted walls
a mural a fragile concern
hanging from a flattened
reserve that says

THIS SPACE HAS BEEN
   WAITING FOR YOU
FOR QUITE SOME TIME

Now what marks
should be made?
Is there a
dove green?

How lonesome
should the reds
become against
the browns?

Where white?

Goose turd green?

Sticks.

Simple sticks.

TOO CLOSE TO THE EYE

Given a song the additive is speech
The blind snake stiffens and spits
A strange look upon the mouth clears
The ancient sounds to make of imitation
Retrieval and provocation one to one
Withered and superfluous to the eye
Carping and rude remedy in the ear
Heartbeat to sabotage the tongue already
Tangled in the teeth and distracted by rhyme
A soundless walk into the mapped hush
One answer too many is the usual proportion
When and where the unheard applies
The harsh perpendicularities of prismatic sounds
An exchange of attractions instead of mossy
Harmonies and the abstracted blend of orthodoxies
Caught on the tongue like a burning rag.

What's substantial?

8 to 10 inches

8 to ten copies

8 to 10 acres

8 to 10 kilos

8 to 10 million

What's substantial?

Who wants to know?

Stubb Crystal, Flinch, Zumzum Demao, Lope, Doc Ceraso, John McNabb, Tasso Rodites, Maurice Ney, Alan Harlock, Ape, Jeff Presseau, Greg Prugh, Murr, Mima Maxey, Tiff, Shales, Claire Odesseys, Mort, Russ Burdock, Chaunce, Bruce Boland, Jay Glover, Shuke, Piz Shinsky, Halfman, Tork, Baby Junior, Galba, Farouk, Everhart Flynnroy, Columbus Chaffin, Xenophon Hassenpflug, Housie, Dominic Marcellus, Mozes, Jaap Radke, Kuku, Istvan, Waves Fredis, Higgy, Two Loaf, Pills Coughlin, La Jeunesse, Teeth Irlbeck, Dinger, Chesky, Hocker, Shinks Perlaky, Jagg Shufflin, Tekoo Woytek, Roach, Clutch Kuscich, Drex, Voice Wachowiak, Kat, Truck Witty, Optima, Bubbles Bast, Ludey Posey, Steve Gump, Elmer, Baby Lammers, Reb Murphy, Freddy Joe Rupert, Yak Hornick, Perma Cute, Mary Rat, Belly Tuso, Saint Sidner, Tribe, Percy Sherrick, Tiny, Jerome Zacker, Numbers Peru, Uriah, Bear, Nicey Niese, Dirtball, Coon Hoelscher, Jape, Keener Wiener, Maw, Pete Teeth, Noot, Worms Hartmann, Nevada Ned, Gutchies, Snuff, Hymer Rhymer, Mouse Reetz, Buck Connors, Perk, Fatty Faeth, Chocho Merkel, Juff, Bone Miller, Diesel Deitz, Winky, Victor Derris, Go Good, Humie Holmes, Dick Bobb, Lungs Mahaffey, Barto, Blue Man, Hilly Jaunckes, Drops Winger, Voodoo Post, Banana Man, Con Rogan, Pilt, Fuse Younes, Brigade, Rennie Ter Kuile, Caliban, Monkeystains, Popear, Logan Loner, Box, Shudds Finke, Del Miner, Schwitzy, Thirty Walks, Harvey Egger, Bent Walzer, Facey Ferace, Weakers, Stashu Buck, Choo Chew McGann, Musty Mohammed, Bud Peck, Louie Keller, Dolph Fein, Cools, Lärm Zwinger, Fem Theurey, Caesar Nucci, Bubba Wickers, Leany Toomes, Jesh, Ohs Minton, Tuffy Wong, Babo Feeney, Nailers, Breath Frankenfield, Lukey Rogers.

Shookie Dull, Tix Deco, Baron Furnace, Quits Genovese, Mel Buffo, Witchy Vickers, Mimmy Kale, Wires Caputo, Perc Kona, Line Caine, Sarge Tillys, Taffy Loon, Yank Pounders, Hazel Hashy, Ironass Dugan, Weepy Flagg, Mooch Kind, Fifty Fixer Taft, Bacon Daub, Cuffy Hayes, Booter Stohl, Napoleon Alcorn, Herk Roeser, Griffey Hooth, Roxie Cochran, Tan Gent Metropolis, Biddy Salter Harlan, Mokes Gavone, Beaks Terwilliger, Fenton Lawbait Walle, Kashee Van Eyck, Toes Maestro, Xanthia Lumens, Ripley Boacks, Cheeks Bunting, Fritzy Tush, Capes Gelman, Nine Ball Howkes, Whitney Toll, Abel Hand, Stiffy Larcomb, Dirk Pettet, Cissie Winder, Nibs Otley, Ben Franz, Tex Emile, Plate Boden, Oscar Spann, Bug Zany, Deaf Sneed, Fuss Dobler, Jon Bottle, Millie Priest, Holes Patroon, Vinnie Pinto, Uppy Merkel, Tip Chimer, Walter Phipps, Calvin Burgart, Dagmar Suares, Radio Rich, Toni Taxi, Bruce Fleegler, Vernon Schaal, Sanders DeHoost, Flash Boroto, Nods, Dickie Beggs, No Nose Tunberg, Oscar Nicolucci, Homer Drumm, Wags Nailer, Fifi Heine, Spags, Willy Clouds, Zebb Heck, End Run, Sparky Parkman, Delbert Hume, Fade X, Gunther, Oklahoma Jones, Buster Figges, Zsa Zsa Landmine Richter, Pastor Mellors, Lark Heaney, Pies Maly, Scarfy Cobbles, Hey Hey Totts, Serge Panto, Cody Samples, Brian Yunker, Long Way Ashton, Chips Quire, Fru Fru Morabito, Ty Clair, Swans Edgerton, Buck Cherches, Mike Bitterice, Horton Khalil, Bozo Fettucca, Hungry Joe, Ricky Pigeons, Lilty, Twigs Preminger, Mabel Shape, Tinks Godfrey, Solomon Twos, Renny Tatum, Robin Spotz, Bolt.

No one to ask: "How are we going to
Pay for all this?" No one to count the unused
Spaces. No one to talk to for days on end
About the unique reflection the trees make
In the frozen lake. No one at all.

So the story can continue. One word at
A time until it falls through the long
Memory and lodges itself like a hyphen between
Some self-congratulatory covenant and a numbing
Assimilation of jettisoned self-correcting promises.

All that remains is blind faith. The slant of ruin and its
Mute interruptions and absentminded stallings,
Vague precept by pendulum and ominous zeros,
The edge of the blade against the glass, pessimistic
Awakenings, hair loss and tooth loss, a hardening

Of the ears: too late to sound any more miserable
Than yourself... no more guesswork just the quick attack
And the tasteless burden of attributes—definitions looking
For the right word to follow. No such luck.
The inescapable intonation left arguing for the exotic.

I mean it I meant it I mean it I meant it
At the same time
I bring the book into the light

A speeding train malachite pillars botany
I mean it I meant it I mean it I meant it
Smokestacks beehives Corinthian columns

I angle the page into the light
I bring the book closer to my eyes I mean it
I meant it I mean it I meant it

Hold this here hold it in place and place it here
This to be held thus to behold in axis of light
And shadow an access of rhythm and motive

January for February, February for March, March for April, April for May, May for June, June for July, July for August, August for September, September for October, October for November, November for December, December for January, January for February, February for March, March for April, April for May, May for June, June for July, July for August, August for September, September for October, October for November, November for December, December for January, January for February for March for April for May for June for July for August for September for October for November for December for January ➡

DIXIE DEUTSCHLAND

Heinz gibt uns **ALMANACH EIN**
Und wir sind so traurig
Heinz gibt uns **ALMANACH ZWEI**
Und was gibt... Ja! ditto... auch traurig
Also schnell zurück kommt **ALMANACH DREI**
Tränen und Tränen und Tränen
Zu letzt kommt **ALMANACH VIER** und **FÜNF**
Jawohl! richtig... gar nichts... nur Tränen
Verflichtsten einmal! sagt Heinz
Kein mehr! sagt Heinz Kein mehr!
Nun haben wir **ALMANACH SECHS** und bald
Kommt **SIEBEN** schwitzt Heinz
Und stirbt kommt am Morgen früh
Man hat was man hat

The reach

In treachery

And the each

In reach

Next point
Lingua franca

Point next
A>B
B>C
C<A
B<A
A+B+C
C-B-A
[Point] [A¹]

Buckshee
Piu mai
Allegro non molto

For [thought through] *aber*
But [stretti]
1 to 5 via 3

The Maori Lines

*Haere mai
Pakeha*

Na waitana?

PAPYRUS 122190. A.

Plato
his hands
the holes
of flow
is this his
half fills
the red poppy
the silver
C-moon
filling shining
meets
the blackness
of purity
by subtraction
creatures
of the inner
sea

FROM POEM TO POEM

Something mooring
In disposition

To make a proportion
And posit it off in words

Broken-off immediate
Thistle down and raven beak

Full of biscuit and suspicions
This is the Silver Age

Any claims against it
Are covered by a multitude of sins

What appears to be nourished by a faith
In what remains of the past ar-tic-u-late

No honor in caution no reparation
In what industry in these wordy matters obliges

Fuck you with your craven doubts
Contra barbaros and cautious praise

Backed into your room full of books
Hunkered *a.k.a.demikos*

1
Odd
The necessary sense

Even
In addition to

2
Maybe might
May be

Might may
Not

3
He she it
Goes out

In the colors
Of speech

4
The Oddments
Mr and Mrs

And their kin
In their skins

Facing pages
February
The month of Februa
Fiber
Whips
Facing pages
Knotted
And woven
The tract
In distraction
And the act
Clear
Of action
On the lea
Of the ear

To define:
To spiral the circle

And echo
The recall

Fine terms
Found

At the finish
But pointing

Back and
Rocking forth

Comes back
The get here

Goes out
The without

To knot
The naught

With not

Wakes apace
and turns
across

Sets along
with parts
from

Comes
and
goes

Trusts in
the imperative
and starts again

I CAN TELL A HAWK FROM A HANDSAW

[ ][ ][ ][ ][ ][ ]
[ ][ ][ ][ ][ ][ ]
[ ][ ][ ][ ][ ][ ]
< >< >< >< >< >< >
< >< >< >< >< >< >
< >< >< >< >< >< >
[ ][ ][ ][ ][ ][ ]
[ ][ ][ ][ ][ ][ ]
[ ][ ][ ][ ][ ][ ]
< >< >< >< >< >< >
< >< >< >< >< >< >
< >< >< >< >< >< >

WHEN THE WIND IS SOUTHERLY

] [] [] [] [] [] [
] [] [] [] [] [] [
] [] [] [] [] [] [
> <> <> <> <> <> <
> <> <> <> <> <> <
> <> <> <> <> <> <
] [] [] [] [] [] [
] [] [] [] [] [] [
] [] [] [] [] [] [
> <> <> <> <> <> <
> <> <> <> <> <> <
> <> <> <> <> <> <

Premise and
muscle

putting one thing
next to another

If given
the choice

of
course

I'd rather
be alive

I can't speak
for you but

who else
needs to know

From I to S
In the making of is
A further 9 pseudomorphic steps
So by omission I is to find
Its way via Phoenicia to
The tooth (pronounced *shin*)
Marked **W** then Σ (σιγμα) in pointing
The passage of years
As is in its present state
And as it stands
Two steps
Past the sum

Note to the Previous

Νεολογος:
Pseudomorphic
To identify by derivative shaping
And "in purpose"
To this specific work
The 9 are J, K, L, M, N, O, P, Q, R
Or the lines that follow
Steps

NOT THE LAST [NEITHER THE FIRST]

How many marks to darken by punctuation [How many marks to darken with punctuation] not what ends as indicated would have it but what is surrounded by an awesome thrift of procedure that calls out its verbal commands by means of a series of overlapping dots dashes circles and the fragmentation and modification of same into arcs barbs flattened ovals extended lines both straight and jagged as well as crosses short lines above short lines and long lines above and below both in addition to certain configurations that begin to resemble letter shapes and at times entire words but as yet no inclination to form sentences can be discerned though the appropriation of entire pages can often be seen in works of ever-increasing interest

Weirs Passage
Bacchus Walk
Huggin Hill
Occupation Road
Wild's Rents
Frying Pan Alley
Ducksfoot Lane
Sheba Street
Crutched Friars
Worlds End Passage
Turk's Row
St. Loo Avenue
Weavers Lane
Herbal Hill
Warlock Road
Pea Hen Court
Turpentine Lane

ONTOLOGY OF A MISSING PART
The day before the day after the day before
The mirrorman reads his meter
Perforated in the affirmative

ONTOLOGY OF A MISSING PART II
Not only the Second Part is missing

ONTOLOGY OF A MISSING PART CONTINUED
The day before the day after the day before
Has finally arrived
It only offers a p.o.v.

ONTOLOGY OF A MISSING PART (MS. STEIN DISCUSSES)
There are in many such ones aspirations and convictions due to quick reactions to others around them, to books they are reading, to the family tradition, to the lack of articulation of the meaning of the being in them that makes them need then to be filled full with other reactions in them so that they will then have something.

ONTOLOGY OF A MISSING PART (MOST RECENT ENTRY)
Part of the Missing Part is under something

BUMPING INTO WALTZERS

A book in the echo

Thank you for
bringing your
states of mind

Orchard
and vineyard

A window
for a door

A twig
of sapling fir
balanced on a nail

How measure
indignation

How express
Why
indignation

Who what

Who's what

A 'Mr Fried Guy' 6 aspirin and coffee black

The smallest accompaniment
built around the future
on behalf of the past

By elephant
to Arcturus

Frightened guesses about the gate

How big a man's chair

The path that approaches

Holding on because bent to the side

The damage to the stone at midword

Approaching like something impossible to find

Too much *what the where*

Too much

The opening a turning

Going for the ace

Marked by that

Dry as the lip

The flange to the rail

As the marks have been put in place

The old scribe with his way of words

Strata and stratagem

No more humoresques

No more alternating aires

Never a humoresque

Never an alternating aire

Couldn't say so

Took
the same

Look
the same

Inside through
the chain

Now

where

a tree

grew

Scorched quartz

And a pot of ink

A new version of Linnaeus

Nails in the music

To terrify
to extrapolate

To extrapolate
to terrify

A VOYAGE TO SATURN

Only a few remaining pages reach the outer rings

The guide gone over
to the guided
Not a betrayal
but no less a matter of occasion

Solar wind and no restaurants

The infinite dilemmas
of the long riff

Red giant

White dwarf

Black sox

The peppermint eagle

The peppermint eagle

What could he have meant

To him it was a kind of currency

The wealth of nations

To be drawn into the matter

By the cold feather

>The ghost of a chance
>The rest of the face
>>To make a perfect fragment

Who's what
That's the imaginary

By what
you time
can you
take me there
By what
is found
in the minimum
take me there
By what
has been lowered
into the voice
take me there
By what
has been raised
by the wind
take me there
By what
remains
of the Eargate and Eyegate
take me there
By what
will be made
of the change
take me there
By what
will be stone
to the one gate
take me there
By what
goes beyond
what would
take me there

So we come to
what we read

Taking in this selection
of what was left behind

Remaking to be seen
what was made to be seen

Has been *locus*
Has been *polis*

Is locus and polis
by r^2 to Times Square

To write the *Pause*

White's white upon white

The hidden house in the hidden page

This that

That would be these

The step is not forward or backward
It's apostrophe . . . separation lacking space
More gesture than movement a numb color
Filling the quid of it as though 'enough' were
The only word the lips and tongue could form
As though yes the no in enough were too prominent

1— the animation of the market

2 — the agreement with other large-brained tool makers

3 — the man plodding toward them

4 — the heart the eye the steer the ocean liner
    in the keyhole

5 — the perhaps and the steps

6 — the tool in the weapon

7 — the classic two-dimensional

8 — the elastic last

9— the emergent claim
    comme l'oiseau du soir

10— the lamp in the color

11—

☞ In the grips and grimace of the animator

An acid cramp
that grinds

An Abigail
As English
As its pollen

Made of the coherence
not coherence-made

A pale Abigail
Moonslough violins
and *ya abeet*

Property
No shelter
Beneath the hard
Below the mulled

The neglected silence

ADDENDA

Ashes and sugary edges

The abandoned news

Glued to the bronze

Nulla dies sine linea
Nulla kicks-off without a line

There was a rumor of a camel in attendance at a hanging at Tyburn—it later proved to be a large deformed horse

The end of A Book in the Echo

Now ... read on ...

Once upon
A time
Just in case

Have you heard
Let me explain
Case in point

No listen
Hey! Hey!
Wait a minute

No really
By the way
Pssst Pssssst

You won't believe
Get a load of this
From my mouth

Listen here
Check this out
I was told

If you ask me

Over the ice
Over the prairie
Under the sod
Ouch ... stones
Chafing tundra
Mammoth meat
And wooly sabered
Bones ... Ouch
Micro-organized
In the macro-sprawl
Forensic runic and
Suspiciously quadruped
Ouch ... there's one
For the pertinacious
Conch-counters
There's another for
The have-you-seeners
Tattooed shale once responsive
To the stains of genesis

MADISON & 59TH

Bruno Paper—thick as a plank. His shoes were sprayed all purple and gold. He had a beautiful motherfuck shirt on. He got it from Switzerland. Last time I saw him he was on the 101 bus to Rikers Island.

Burnt Njal pronounced burdened jowl–
aka Burton Jewel–

Gorgeous and shattered–
who are we
when the snow melts ... the snows melt?

Our fingers twisting some *oid*-substance
from the nostrils ...

Welcome, foreigner.

From whom are we?

Who wants to know?

QUESTION EVERY CONTEXT [TOTAL RECALL]

A voice an interior at its discretion
Devotion and circumstance
Parts of the dimension
Leaving behind the reply
To the answer
The reply to the answer

Confined by the weight of relief
Silence metallic
Building a presence apart
And not so much sustained
As arrived at again
Too much too little too late

Much that is
Does not
But by chance

To be
We may
That soon

Either this
Is how or this
Is neither

Yet there always
Seems to be
One next and one

To be
Enough as
Another

Into our newly
From that which
Still will come

To be or that
Much that can
And does not

Three reasoned interiors

The door is in half

The door is in-half

The door is in half

Three reasoned exteriors

The door is in-half

The door is in half

The door is in-half

Traction to subvert
The billions grabbed
Warped in the wolf

Does notion of develop
Equate with extension
Out of the hold

Out of the grasp of
Ve- vel- velo and lop
Off- off of- and out

Decim- decem- ex-
The absorption of words
Not immersion

(The parenthetical moves
(within to develop clarity
not merely make clear)))

Wild dissolves
Complaints
Of departure

How wild
How dissolved
How departed

Through
The door in-half
Or the door in half

How complains through
The door in-half
In half

Where words may be used to reason and measure at the edges of their scale and proportion. At is the thin edge———————————————with blunts.

THE AGONY OF CARBON

The trunk turns
and the torque
is change by
subtraction

Cold as the door
that closed to bring
focus to the moonlight
and fatten the surface

The parchment hearth
holds the dim light
and blocks the heat
that retains its glow

A shield of clock-faces stuck on

Where

Where the head begins
This dry configuration

Where

A shield of clock-faces stuck on
Any
Pause
Where
A shield of clock-faces would be chronic
In its legible traces

Where the head ends
And the eyes in the face begin

Which

Which face

Faces

What is sung
brings mixed feelings
the words aren't
right for the notes
and sometimes, per-
haps most often,
the notes aren't
right for the music
and to hell with
the words. But
with this carcass
of sound a meal
the size of an opera
has often been prepared.

Some days remain empty, cold and fragile
Some days just remain
The empty, cold and fragile ones
Have been given you
In default of a less suitable sense of
The self-conciliatory and the wish
To think you have enough on your plate
When you damn well know you don't

FIASCO ZIG-ZAG
NO ESCAPE FROM THE NOESCOPE

Shines down the doublet
And jumps in the eye

Hello, Citizen

Episode of The Sheen

The purest glare
Out of the light

Is it there
Or is it what they do
Purest
Out of the light

Just a variant luster
To be taken

Hello, Comrade

I've come for you

While you're pure
And no shadow holds

ROLL X THE X ROLE

Below 41° an under-inked series of letters
and bars in red and black further
overprinted with random words and letters
low gloss puns through three languages
Russian English and Italian notched
along their respective consonants to resemble
birds in flight over monkeys in trees and
fierce grinning women waiting for love
Non-articulated acoustics radiophonics
and the typographic word for horizon
The elemental variety of so many directions at once

Reno Huxley
I come before
Darwin and
That kept me
Very busy

Paradise Darwin
I come and go after
Huxley and
Make plans with all
That time on my hands

Reno Darwin signs
For Paradise Huxly [sic]

Salt

But the ideas
Come from sugar

Sugar and almonds—
Panforte scuro

And when there is
No more
All that can be done
Is walk up to
And wait

Another use
For the hieratic torsions
Of the face

New York City,
November-December, 1990
February, 1991
September 1-17, 1994

Potes & Poets Press, Inc.
181 Edgemont Avenue
Elmwood, CT 06110

POTES AND POETS PRESS PUBLICATIONS

Gilbert Adair, *Upstate Stoic*
Mickal And, Book 7, *Samsara Congeries*
Bruce Andrews, *Blue Horizon*
Bruce Andrews, *Excommunicate*
Bruce Andrews, *Executive Summary*
Bruce Andrews, from *Shut Up*
Rae Armantrout, from *Made to Seem*
Todd Baron, *dark as a hat*
Dennis Barone, *The World / The Possibility*
Dennis Barone, *Forms / Froms*
Dennis Barone, *New.ark*
Dennis Barone, *The Book of Discoveries*
D. Barone/P. Ganick, eds, *The Art of Practice: 45 Contemporary Poets*
Lee Bartlett, *Red Scare*
Beau Beausoleil, *in case / this way two things fall*
Martine Bellen, *Places People Dare Not Enter*
Steve Benson, *Reverse Order*
Steve Benson, *Two Works Based on Performance*
Brita Bergland, *form is bidden*
Charles Bernstein, *Amblyopia*
Charles Bernstein, *Conversation with Henry Hills*
Julia Blumenreich, *Parallelism*
David Bromige, *Romantic Traceries*
Lee Ann Brown, *Velocity City*
Paul Buck, *No Title*
Gerald Burns, *Seventeen Poems*
John Byrum, *Cells*
O. Cadiot / C. Bernstein, *Red, Green & Black*
Abigail Child, *A Motive for Mayhem*
A. Clarke / R. Sheppard, eds., *Floating Capital*
Norman Cole, *Metamorphopsia*
Clark Coolidge, *The Symphony*
Cid Corman, *Essay on Poetry*
Cid Corman, *Root Song*
Beverly Dahlen, *A Reading (11-17)*
Tina Darragh, *a(gain)2st the odds*
Tina Darragh, *Exposed Faces*
Alan Davies, *a an av es*
Alan Davies, *Mnemonotechnics*
Alan Davies, *Riot Now*
Jean Day, *The I and the You*
Jean Day, from *No Springs Trail*
Ray DiPalma, *The Jukebox of Memnon*
Ray DiPalma, *New Poems*
Ray DiPalma, *14 Poems from Metropolitan Corridor*
Johanna Drucker, *Three Early Fictions*
Rachel Blau DuPlessis, *Drafts #8 and #9*
Rachel Blau DuPlessis, *Drafts 3-14*
Rachel Blau DuPlessis, *Tabula Rosa*
Johanna Drucker, from *Bookscape*
Theodore Enslin, *Case Book*
Theodore Enslin, *Meditations on Varied Grounds*
Theodore Enslin, *September's Bonfire*
Elaine Equi, from *Decoy*
Norman Fischer, from *Success*
Norman Fischer, *The Devices*
Steven Forth, *Calls This*
Kathleen Fraser, *Giotto : Arena*
Peter Ganick, *likely to this*
Peter Ganick, *Met Honest Stanzas*
Peter Ganick, *Rectangular Morning Poem*
Peter Ganick, *Two Space Six*
Susan Gevirtz, *Korean and Milkhouse*
Susan Gevirtz, *Prosthesis :: Caesarea*

Robert Grenier, *What I Believe*
Jessica Grim, *It / Ohio*
Jefferson Hansen, *Three Poems*
Carla Harryman, *Vice*
Carla Harryman, *The Words*
Crag Hill, *Leap Yea*
Susan Howe, *Federalist 10*
Janet Hunter, *in the absence of alphabets*
P. Inman, *backbite*
P. Inman, *Think of One*
P. Inman, *waver*
Andrew Levy, *Reading Places, Reading Times*
Andrew Levy, from *salvage device plants*
Lori Lubeski, from *You Torture Me*
Steve MacCaffery, from *Theory of Sediment*
Jackson Mac Low, *Prose & Verse from the Early 80's*
Jackson Mac Low, *Twenties (8-25)*
Barbara Moraff, *Learning to Move*
Laura Moriarty, *the goddess*
Sheila E. Murphy, *Literal Ponds*
Susan Smith Nash, *Liquid Babylon*
Susan Smith Nash, *Scenes from Hollywood Babylon*
Melanie Neilson, *Civil Noir*
Janette Orr, *The Balcony of Escape*
Jena Osman, *Ellerby's Observatory*
Gil Ott, *Public Domain*
Maureen Owen, *Imaginary Income*
Maureen Owen, *Untapped Maps*
Rochelle Owens, from *Luca*
Bob Perelman, *Two Poems*
Nick Piombino, from *The Frozen Witness*
Larry Price, *Work in Progress*
Keith Rahmings, *Printouts*
Dan Raphael, *The Matter What Is*
Dan Raphael, *Oops Gotta Go*
Dan Raphael, *Zone du Jour*
Stephen Ratcliffe, *Sonnets*
Stephen Ratcliffe, *spaces in the light said to be where one/ comes from*
Joan Retallack, *Western Civ Cont'd*
Maria Richard, *Secondary Image / Whisper Omega*
Susan Roberts, *cherries in the afternoon*
Susan Roberts, *dab / a calling in*
Kit Robinson, *The Champagne of Concrete*
Kit Robinson, *Up early*
Leslie Scalapino, *clarinet part I heard*
Leslie Scalapino, *Goya's L.A.*
Leslie Scalapino, *How Phenomena Appear to Unfold*
Laurie Schneider, *Pieces of Two*
Spencer Selby, *Accident Potential*
Spencer Selby, *House of Before*
Gail Sher, *w/*
James Sherry, *Lazy Sonnets*
Ron Silliman, *B A R T*
Ron Silliman, *Lit*
Ron Silliman, from *Paradise*
Ron Silliman, *Toner*
Margy Sloan, from *On Method*
Juliana Spahr, *Identifying*
Pete Spence, *Almanak*
Pete Spence, *Elaborate at the Outline*
Thomas Taylor, *The One, The Same, and The Other, 7-9*
Liz Waldner, *The Way You May*
Rosmarie Waldrop, *Cornered Stones / Split Infinities*
Diane Ward, *Being Another / Locating in the World*
Diane Ward, *Crossing*
Diane Ward, *Imaginary Movie*
Craig Watson, *The Asks*
Craig Watson, *Drum*
Barret Watten, from *Two Recent Works*
Hannah Weiner, *Nijole's House*
Matt Wellick, *Imperial Mind*